T0065315

Visits *with* Mom

A Journey Through Time and Beyond

LORI SZEPELAK

BALBOA
PRESS
A DIVISION OF HAY HOUSE

Balboa Press books may be ordered through booksellers or by contacting:

Balboa Press
A Division of Hay House
1663 Liberty Drive
Bloomington, IN 47403
www.balboapress.com
1 (877) 407-4847

Print information available on the last page.

ISBN: 978-1-9822-0678-9 (sc)
ISBN: 978-1-9822-0679-6 (e)

Balboa Press rev. date: 07/02/2018

The author with her mother.

This book is dedicated to my mother, Thelma Josephson, who passed away in 2008. She continues to be my inspiration because of her unconditional love - which remains constant in my life.

Also ... thank you to:

- *Hay House for believing in this message from Heaven ...*

- *My niece Donna McLean for her beautiful depiction of angel wings used in this book ...*

- *My guardian angels for their love and guidance ... and*

- *All of the beautiful Energy and Light in the Universe. I send out gratitude every day for the blessings I have received and the ability to share these messages with others across Mother Earth.*

Contents

Introduction

The author with her parents on Christmas eve.

Mom was my best friend.

Mom's shoulders were always there to lean on or cry on - with no judgment.

The 49 years I had her by my side were precious and I knew how blessed I was to have learned so much about family, faith, and life from her.

This book is dedicated to the one woman who meant everything to me - who gave me life - and her love - unconditionally.

Since her passing, she has continued to share her love for me in boundless ways - ways I could have never imagined.

These pages reflect my journey with my mom and how visits over the years shaped the person I am today.

Looking back at all of the visits with mom over the years - I realize those conversations helped to shape my spiritual journey which would ultimately result in being open to what the Universe offers to all of us.

I hope my journey will inspire you to take a more in-depth look at your spiritual path and perhaps see how the people closest to you will always be there for you - whether on Earth or on another spiritual plane.

I also hope sharing these visits with my mom open your heart to what is possible and that you share this message with others so we can have a profound impact on humanity.

What the world needs now more than ever is love - may your journey be filled with abundant love from your mom - and the Source of all the beautiful love and Light in the Universe.

CHAPTER 1

The Early Years

Growing up in the 1960's in a small town was a gift in itself.

The town of Russell, Massachusetts, is nestled along the Westfield River and my dad, Francis Josephson, was fortunate to have a job working in one of the three paper mills that supported the many families in the town and surrounding communities.

Dad's work in the "beater room" at the Westfield River Paper Company ensured a steady income so Mom chose to stay at home. Since Dad had to adhere to a schedule of 7-3, 3-11, and 11-7 shifts, Mom was always at the ready if I needed help with homework assignments, scrapped knees or to be an avid listener when life seemed to be so complicated.

Every school day had a flow - Mom would wake up early for her cup of coffee and then start preparing breakfast so that when my alarm went off, all I had to do was jump up, get dressed, and head for the kitchen where the delicious aroma of French toast smothered with butter and maple syrup or scrambled eggs and cinnamon toast awaited me at the table.

During breakfast we would have a quick chat about my day and hers - and Mom would always ask me what I wanted for dinner. Mom, having grown up during the Great Depression, specialized in meat and potato recipes and her go-to meals ranged from Beef Stew and Hamburg Gravy (my Dad's favorite), to one of my ultimate favorites - Chicken and Dumplings.

As I write and picture those small slices of Americana - I wish I appreciated those moments more that now are cherished memories.

After breakfast I sped out the door - with Mom waiting with a brown lunch bag to hand off. Each lunch was a surprise but mostly consisted of peanut butter sandwiches which could keep for hours in my locker.

I always glanced back as I left the driveway since Mom was still standing in the doorway waving goodbye. If only I could relive one day to experience that joy again - simple acts of love that we take for granted.

When the last day of school arrived before summer vacation, there were always a few tears shed since I knew there would be classmates I wouldn't see for months. Of course, since summer days seemed endless, soon the kids in my neighborhood were excited to again start exploring the mountains that surrounded our tiny town.

Summer also meant taking off for the day on our bikes and our parents did not have to worry about us. Among our stops would be the Russell Library, the mountain spring for a refreshing drink of water, the ice cream shop with its penny candy counter, and the Russell Pool.

Our town was fortunate to have an Olympic-size pool and lifeguards and all the kids flocked there every afternoon. Once we staked out a spot for our towels on the cement - we couldn't wait to jump into the crystal clear water to cool off. Life was good.

Since accessing a phone was a difficult task, Mom would give me an approximate time to return for dinner - and a clock at the pool or the library were ways I could ensure I wouldn't be late.

While I was out with friends, most days Mom would be visiting with friends from the neighborhood or my sister Joyce would visit from Blandford and the two would enjoy a quick trip to Westfield - the closest city. When Mom returned - she always had bags overflowing with groceries and always bought extra foodstuffs so she could pass them on to my two sisters and their young families.

From an early age Mom taught me about the importance of giving to others - whether it was the neighborhood children who needed a bite to eat because their parents both worked - or to family members who had limited incomes.

Mom had such a big heart - I now understand how much pleasure she received when giving to others.

CHAPTER 2

On My Own

The author visiting her mom.

During and after college, there were calls every day to Mom to touch base, to update her on my trials and tribulations, and to hear her caring voice and advice. Mom's advice was always spot on - even though there were times I didn't agree when I sought her counsel.

When I started working full-time at the local daily newspaper, my schedule required arriving at 6 a.m. and Mom was always waiting at 5:45 by the phone for my call to say hi. I never knew what the day ahead would entail, so hearing Mom's reassuring words of "you can do anything you put your mind and heart to" was a godsend.

In those early years, there were editors I admired and learned from, but one constant influence was Mom reminding me I was in a role that God wanted me to be doing at that moment in time.

My years at the newspaper passed quickly and one important lesson I learned from my first editor - Gene Casey - was "There is a story around every corner and it is your job to find it!"

I have always treasured that message and like that lesson - there is a message for each of us around every corner and we need to listen intently with an open mind and heart to recognize it when it touches us.

Mom loved hearing about my days on deadline working the paste-up boards, interviewing people, and capturing their essence in a photograph. She was a newspaper subscriber and waited patiently for the paperboy to deliver her copy knowing I had a small part in its contents.

As the years passed between fruitful relationships and excursions with girlfriends, Mom and Dad always looked forward to my visits. I would give them an approximate arrival time and Dad would be standing in the doorway - patiently waiting.

The three of us would gather at the round wooden kitchen table, and I would share the intricacies of the day. Dad would sit quietly and listen mostly to the conversation, but before I left he always asked for a foot massage. I always obliged.

On occasion my Mom and my sisters would take off for day trips or overnight bus trips but because I was so new to the workforce I seldom took time off and missed quality time with them. Those missed getaways are among the many regrets I carry in my heart.

As time passed, I did start taking trips - mostly with girlfriends - and realized that my best friend - Mom - might also be a fun traveling partner.

One of our best trips was a few summer days spent in Ogunquit, Maine. We stayed in a motel and explored the town and beach each day and every evening we had dinner at a restaurant recommended by someone we met earlier in the day. On our last night I wanted to surprise her with a ticket to the theater and we saw *Music Man* at the Ogunquit Playhouse which is on the U.S. National Register of Historic Places.

Even though that night was more than 30 years ago as I write this chapter, I can see us vividly sitting in those comfy seats ready for the play to start, and then breaking out in smiles as the Music Man himself - "Professor Harold Hill" - strolled down the aisle greeting all of us as residents of "River City, Iowa."

On the trip home we took an alternate route and enjoyed a more carefree ride looking at the scenic mountains and chatting away. What comes to mind remembering that drive is pure delight!

It doesn't matter if it is a day or a week's sojourn with your mom - spend the time while you can - and relish every moment.

While I spent a few other day trips with Mom - including a dance recital at Jacob's Pillow in Becket, Massachusetts - I have many regrets of not suggesting more excursions.

As the years passed, Mom had sporadic health issues which required stays in hospitals and nursing homes since assisted living centers were still years away.

Mom had a strong constitution and would fight through any ailment - then return home a stronger woman. Those visits in the hospitals and nursing homes would often follow a hectic work day. Many times I was tired and wanted to go home to unwind but the car always found its way to her because she too had a full day of rehabilitation and needed to see a familiar face for encouragement.

As soon as I walked in her room - she lit up with a huge

smile - and stretched her arms out to me to give me a big hug. How I miss those embraces!

During Mom's final months, she sensed her time to pass was drawing near. She would confide in me that she was tired and knew she wouldn't be around for another Christmas. My heart sank.

Since I sensed her will weakening I spent more evenings with her. Before I tapped on her window to let her know of my arrival, I topped off her bird feeder. When she saw me she would clasp her hands together in delight - not only knowing the birds wouldn't go hungry - but I was there to see her and share the day's experiences.

Spending time on Mother's Day was especially poignant over the years and never knowing if a particular Mother's Day would be the last time you would share that special time together, the celebration always consisted of a loving card and a small gift - but what Mom sought more than anything was time with her daughters and her grandchildren. Even though she would be showered with bouquets of flowers and affectionate placards conveying a grandmother's love - it was still the time spent talking that she cherished the most.

Her birthdays were also special gatherings and her favorite was when dear friends and extended family turned out for her 90th birthday celebration. We had reserved the conference room in the nursing home and decorated it with colorful balloons - and the room was jam-packed with staff, family and friends - bearing gifts and a lot of hugs and kisses. I couldn't remember a time in the recent past when

Mom had been so happy. After she unwrapped her presents and cut her cake - she shared a poem (Author Unknown) she had discovered that captured how she felt on her special day. The poem read in part:

Today, dear Lord, I am 80 and there's much I haven't done.
I hope dear Lord you'll let me live until I'm 81.
But then if I haven't finished all I want to do,
Would you let me stay a while until I am 82?
So many places I want to go, so very much to see.
Do you suppose you could manage to make it 83?
And if by then I am still alive,
I'd like to stay until 85.

Mom did receive her wish - she lived past 90 - and up until her last few weeks she was reading a book a day and chatting away with her visitors. Mom so loved life and wanted the best for everyone she knew. She prayed a lot during breaks from her reading and relished the times when nursing home staffers would meander in to check on her and she would always engage them in conversation - asking them about their families. She had a quick wit and a sharp mind which was a blessing for all of us.

If you still have time to spend with your mom - take the time to make her day. Whether it is a phone call or dropping in to surprise her - know you will always be welcomed with open arms.

A mom's love is unconditional - she nurtured you from the time you were conceived - and she will always love you (and worry about you). That is what a mom does!

CHAPTER 3

The Last Days

My mom was an avid reader - she enjoyed books on spirituality - and romance - and prided herself in reading a book a day. I would often suggest she attend a program at the nursing home in between her reading and her remark was always the same - "I don't want to sit with those old people!"

At 93, she still thought of herself as youthful - and she was certainly young at heart. What a gift Spirit blessed her with!

When we received a call one morning that she was being rushed to the ER - it made no sense to us. We had seen her the day before and she was fine. I was at work and quickly made the trip - luckily only 20 minutes - to the ER where I met my sister. Mom was on a stretcher and was being hooked up to all sorts of tubes. Why? I started to cry and as I turned away I saw her gaze at me before she was sedated.

What we learned was she was suffering from aspiration

pneumonia - brought on by a nurse who didn't administer Mom's medications properly which caused her to choke.

How could such a thing happen? We immediately alerted the state Department of Public Health and insisted on an investigation. If this happened to Mom - it could certainly happen to others.

In the two weeks that followed - our mother's will to live remained strong.

As days passed physicians decided to keep Mom sedated - and only resuscitated her to keep her abreast of her condition and to allow her to make her own decisions. We spent days sitting by her side - holding her hand - not even sure if she knew we were there.

After almost two weeks of this type of treatment - which seemed barbaric - physicians said her only relief would be a tracheotomy. Mom didn't hesitate and said yes to the surgery. When the surgery was over, the surgeon said he almost lost her once during the procedure and was amazed at her age that she came through the surgery without complications.

What the surgeon didn't explain to her is that a huge, obnoxious oxygen machine would be pulling on her throat and causing such agony with every breath. Physicians did not explain to her (or us) how her life would improve with other technology available but instead led Mom to believe this would be her life going forward. The physicians also kept her drugged and would only revive her for a few minutes to talk to her and then they would send her back into a coma state.

I have so many regrets looking back - why didn't we as a family ask more questions? Why didn't we question the process that the physicians put her through? It breaks my heart every time I relive those tortuous days.

As the days progressed I visited Mom in the ICU after work each day and one day she told me that the Virgin Mother had come to her and said it was "Ok to go."

Mom always prayed to Our Lady throughout her life and always trusted that her prayers were being answered.

I didn't tell Mom that earlier that day I had stopped to St. Mary's Church in Westfield and prayed to Our Lady for guidance. There are beautiful statues in the church's lower level and I have found great comfort several times over the years there when you can be alone with your thoughts and prayers.

Mom said Our Lady was "beautiful" and I knew in my heart that all of our prayers were being answered - even though it might not be the resolution we sought.

A few days later on a Sunday morning, I had gone to work to catch up on paperwork and my sister called and said Mom had decided to end her life. It was a devastating message for all of us. Within an hour we all gathered at Mom's bedside in the ICU, and spent the next 23 hours holding her hands and telling her how much she was loved.

After she passed, my sister and I left the hospital and each of us headed for our homes. I decided to stop for a newspaper to catch up on the news and as I opened the car door I found a penny on the ground by my feet. I knew it was the first sign from Mom - how she loved the story of pennies from Heaven.

CHAPTER 4

An Angel On My Shoulder

A blue aura among the trees.

The most profound gift Mom gave me after her passing was a photograph taken the day after her funeral.

Earlier in the day, my husband could see how distraught I was and he had an idea - let's take a hike in the woods. Our destination was a small town in the Berkshires called Hancock - and just before we stepped off on the hike - I looked up at Mom - I told her how much I loved her, how much I missed her, but knew she was in a better place. I asked her in the moment if she would join me on the hike.

What transpired from that hike was a photo that changed my life - and how I see the "Other Side" making connections with us on the earth plane.

When Mom came through and I saw her image in a blue aura amongst a beautiful setting of trees, I realized that love transcends time and space and she had found a way to let me know she was with me.

Over the years she had told me that once she made it on the "other side," she would find a way to let me know her spirit was free and flying high. I always joked to her that I couldn't imagine how she would be able to pull that off but she assured me nothing was impossible when it came to God, the angels, and the beautiful love of the Universe.

What I have come to realize is that Mom passed on so many lessons over the years and I wasn't aware or "awake" enough to appreciate them.

As I shared that photograph with family and friends, many

asked me if I would photograph them because they too had lost someone they loved with all of their heart. I have to admit that request felt daunting because I knew how much a photograph would mean to each person - and not surprisingly - everyone received an amazing gift of love which took many different forms - in auras, hearts, and orbs.

As my spiritual journey kicked into high gear I felt called by my guardian angels to write *An Angel On My Shoulder* and not only include my story but also the stories of others who I had photographed.

While I expected that several individuals might have said they would prefer to keep their photo and story private - everyone I asked didn't hesitate - the answer was yes. The consensus was if their photo could lift someone else's heart - it would be worth it. What a gift of love that was and another lesson for me to learn about feeling confident and comfortable to ask others to touch the hearts of people around the globe.

As I put the finishing touches on the book and then waited for my first set of books to be printed, I questioned myself again - was this what my angels wanted?

I had attended an angel reading program a year earlier and had been given a message to "pursue my photography because my photographs would help others heal." Did I interpret the message correctly?

How I knew for sure that I was on the right path was a message from the angels in a most unexpected way.

On Dec. 12, 2010, I started to write a press release about my forthcoming book and typed a headline in bold - "*Southampton Woman Self Publishes Book on Guardian Angels.*" I took a short while to write the release, saved the file, and then reviewed it. Having worked in the newspaper field for more than 30 years, I realized immediately that was a boring headline. I assured myself if I just wait for a few minutes something clever would come to mind.

After several minutes waiting for some inspiration - nothing transpired. More than 10 minutes passed - still no clever headline came to fruition. As I sat at my home desk, I gazed up at my angels and said, "We have come a long way in the past year. I could have never imagined that in a few days this book would be available to not only help others - but for individuals to also pass on to lift the hearts of people they know. However, in this moment, I feel like I am letting you down because I can't get a good headline for this press release."

As my heart sank ... I turned away from my computer and worked on some paperwork. Within a moment or two I felt a need to "look back at my computer screen." As I did - I saw that the bold headline was much longer than I had remembered typing. I read it again - "*Southampton Woman Self Publishes Book on Guardian Angels - Because Her Angels Asked Her To.*"

Wow! How did they add those words?

I stared upward and cried. I told my angels I didn't know

how they manipulated that headline but that message would definitely get an editor's attention. The headline was perfect!

What I also realized in that moment was my angels knew I needed to start sharing the messages without any doubts in my mind or heart. With those few words - all of the questions I had faded away and I have never turned back.

I thanked them many times for that gift and love sharing that story with others because it shows how much our angels care about us - and always want what is best for our higher good.

So many lessons to learn - and I had to learn to wait and listen for the signs.

My wish for you is that your spiritual journey will be abundant with the many blessings of those who love (and have loved) you - and when your day arrives to continue on the "other side," you too will come back and share your love with others so their journey will be blessed.

In this way, we will all be a part of the loving energy that makes this Universe possible.

CHAPTER 5

Astral Travels With Mom

Do you have vivid memories of your mom - or are you still blessed to have her in your life?

I believe many of us would welcome the chance for one more hug, one more kiss, and one more time to say "I love you."

I know I do.

One lesson my Mom taught me from the other side is that anything is possible.

How?

"Believe!"

When my husband and I returned from Mom's funeral, I

had several vases of beautiful flowers that were given to me and wanted to find the perfect settings for each one. Our living room has an open floor plan with an adjoining dining room so with ample light coming in from the backyard - I knew these two rooms would be perfect backdrops.

As I was placing the first arrangement on a glass table in the living room - my eyes caught a glance of something moving next to the glass doors - it was a beautiful, rolling circle of light.

How could that be? I had never seen anything like that clear sphere but there it was. My eyes followed the sphere for only a few seconds as it danced across the living room into the dining room - and then just as fast as it appeared - it was gone.

My husband wasn't in the room so I couldn't ask him if he had seen the beautiful manifestation of light. Of course, I knew that Mom had to find a way to help me make a connection with her because she could see how sad I was. That sphere of light - which lit me up inside - was such a blessing for my heart. I knew it had to be Mom and I thanked her for that gift which is one of many that I treasure.

Since Mom's passing, she has visited me in a variety of ways, but one of the most profound mechanisms is through my dreams.

I never have any idea when Mom will make an appearance - but I can assure you - when she does it is a grand entrance!

One night several years after she passed, I felt her presence hovering above me as I slept - and I could clearly see her face but her body was like rubber. I cupped my hands around her face and kissed her. We spoke without any words being said - because you are able to communicate through each other's Spirit and Soul. I told her I loved her and I saw her mouth move to say "I love you too." As I embraced the love she was emitting - I wanted to continue to hold her but she was slowly disappearing.

I was startled from the experience and awoke to my German shepherd barking and getting up on our bed - since she too sensed Mom's presence. My dog may appear to be a sound sleeper but she is very much in tune to other energy and couldn't stop barking - wanting to protect me. I reassured her everything was Ok and she had experienced an otherworldly exchange. After a few moments she relaxed and retreated to her cushion at the foot of our bed.

I enjoy sharing my moments in time with Mom with others who are open to the possibilities of what the Universe offers us because those moments are so vivid and brimming with love.

The catalyst for this book was sealed on the early morning of Dec. 8, 2016, when I awoke from a dream that left me at first with such joy and then trembling with tears due to the extraordinary experience.

As soon as I awoke at 6:18 a.m. I scrambled to find a notepad and pen to write down every detail I could remember from the encounter with Mom.

The dream started as I joined my sister Bonnie walking along a stone path that was adjacent to a manicured sprawling lawn on a picturesque bay.

The dream took an odd turn when my sister motioned to me to look ahead at the person on a riding lawnmower and then Bonnie bowed her head and knelt to the ground.

As I watched my sister kneel - which was unrealistic due to her recent hip replacement surgery - I knew I needed to investigate.

As I approached the woman on the lawnmower I soon realized it was Mom and I ran to her.

She was encased on the lawnmower by a steel cage but yet there were openings to squeeze through so I asked her if I could get closer. Mom said - "Only for a moment."

After several body contortions to get into the encasement area, I was able to put my arms around Mom and told her how much I loved her. I also asked her to tell Dad how much I loved and missed him too. As we talked no words were actually exchanged - or needed - we could read each other's thoughts and communicate without talking. I could also feel how holy she was.

As I held her for those brief seconds, Mom slowly became fluid - pulsating with light, energy, and love. Also, what was different from other visitations, I could see she was made up of stars - and they shone so brightly - I was mesmerized by the sight.

Since she was slowly fading away in front of my eyes - I had the chance to ask her some questions. The first question was "What is Heaven like?" and Mom looked up with a big beautiful smile to the sky and said it was "beautiful."

After I wrote down all of the details from the questions I asked, I slipped back into bed and my husband asked me what happened. As I recounted the dream I immediately started to shutter and couldn't stop crying while my husband held me. He wanted to comfort me and I explained I was Ok - that I needed to release all of the emotions I experienced from the encounter.

As my husband returned to his slumber, I heard the words "Visits With Mom" and sensed that would be the title of my third book.

As I lay in bed, I thanked Mom, not only for the magnificent gift - but especially since it was just before Christmas - and I prayed that her gift would one day inspire and comfort others.

CHAPTER 6

Loving Reminders

The author on right with her sister Bonnie, niece Donna, and her mother Thelma, on a day at the beach.

For those readers who are still fortunate to have your mom in your life … here are some loving thoughts to consider:

- Tell your mom how much you love her - every day.
- If you live away from home, call your mom as often as possible - even if it is only to say hi. You will sense the huge smile that will grace her face as she hears your voice (or with social media - text her, email her - it is the thought that counts).
- If you are in your mom's presence - give her a big hug.
- Before your mom asks you how your day was - ask her what was special about her day.
- Surprise your mom periodically with a small, thoughtful gift (fresh flowers, one rose, a framed photo of the two of you, a copy of the book she has hinted she would like to read but seems to never have the time to pick up).
- For special occasions including Mother's Day or your mom's birthday, how do you celebrate them? Know that your mom isn't in need of more gifts - your presence is a gift in itself. Time spent cooking her favorite meal for her or watching a movie she always enjoyed seeing are simple ways to let her know you are paying attention to the little details that make her happy.
- Taking a drive with mom can also be an uplifting way to spend time together. Is there a new restaurant that specializes in your mom's favorite foods? Surprise her by taking her on a whirlwind afternoon of lunch and catching up. Does she like a glass of wine from time to time? Local wineries are flourishing and many offer delicious appetizer platters which in itself can make fabulous picnic.
- Your mom will also relish spending time with your children so include them in your plans from time time. What activities will everyone enjoy? From walki

on the beach to visiting a museum - what special memories can you think of creating that will leave an indelible impression on everyone?

- If your mom is more limited in her abilities to get out and about - have you thought of ways to bring nature closer to her? My mom loved bird feeders and bird houses because she could see nature unfold outside of her window. She would revel in talking about the visitors she had - especially in spring when many of the familiar birds of New England would once again reappear and find their way to her sanctuary. Since my mom was in a wheelchair during the last years of her life - and was a bit self-conscious about it - we tried to find avenues where she felt like she blended in.

- A favorite trip for my mom was returning to her hometown and stopping in at the homes of her longtime friends. Since her friends were also limited to where they could travel to - driving to their homes was a blessing. Those conversations where old friends could reminisce and share their stories were priceless.

- If traveling back to your mom's hometown isn't feasible, suggest a trip around the community where she currently resides. Each town has its own distinct attributes and it is important to support local businesses. A walk down Main Street with quaint shops can be a welcome sight instead of the hustle and bustle of busy mega malls.

- Before you end your day - give gratitude for your mother's love - and tell her how much she means to you. Can you imagine the wonderful night's rest your mom will have after your last-minute exchange?

- Giving gratitude is an important part of our lives as we travel this earthly plane. One day - when we return to Divine love on the astral plane - we will be able to look back and know in our hearts how much love we created and sent out to make a difference in the world. I can't think of a better gift to give our loved ones - and the planet.

For those of you who have lost your mom - there are ways to reconnect. Try these suggestions:

- Say hi first thing in the morning to her - out loud, through a whisper, or touching an heirloom that she passed down to you.
- Throughout the day - look up at Heaven and acknowledge her presence is among all of the Divine love in the Universe.
- If prayer was an important part of your mom's life - perhaps read aloud a favorite prayer of hers - asking her to join you by your side and as you recite intently - feel her loving presence surrounding you.
- Did your mom give you a book she wanted you to read but you never seemed to have time? Did you save that book? Maybe take a few minutes each night - in a quiet space - to read it and thank her for the gift of that time you are spending together.
- If you have downtime - waiting in traffic, watching your pasta cook in a pot of bubbling water, or any other myriad ways you can think of - let your mom know you are thinking of her. Even though she continues on her

own spiritual journey - part of her journey includes the love she has for you which is unending.

- If you have a family of your own, how much do they know about their grandmother? Do you have a special album with family photos that you can recount family memories? Have you kept a journal that you will be able to pass on? Do you have home movies that can be viewed during a family night - sharing the memories that you cherish so they are passed on to the next generation?

- As you close your eyes at the end of the day, say goodnight to mom and thank her for the life she gave you. Despite the trials and tribulations of each day, she carried you all those years ago because she knew how special you would be in this world.

CHAPTER 7

My sacred space

Graphic of angel wings.

I have a sacred space in my home with beautiful gemstones and crystals including Angelite and Rose Quartz, pendulums, angel cards and special family photos. Also, a sacred crystal healing grid with Guardian Angel rutilated quartz graces the room that creates a strong vortex of Life Force energy.

It is in this special space - when the house is quiet and I have a few moments to meditate and ask questions to Mom, the Angels, and the Universe - I find the most peace.

Over the years I have reached for my angel cards - when I was sad, when I sought a message, when I needed to look inward. I have never been disappointed.

My favorite cards, created by Doreen Virtue and James Van Praagh, are called *"Talking To Heaven."* The process is simple - ask a question, shuffle the cards, and wait for a card (or two!) to stand out from the rest. In some cases, my cards have literally flown across the room or fallen to the floor - a sure sign that the card was meant to be read at that moment in time.

I started working on this book in December 2016 but found myself a few months later questioning myself again on whether I was on track - is this the book I am supposed to be writing? As always, the messages come through loud and clear!

On April 3, 2017, I decided to seek guidance from Mom and turned to my angel cards. Earlier in the day I had found three pennies so I thought that was a good omen (since I was working on my third book). I asked her - am I on the right track for my third book? A card immediately turned up that indicated Mom had become one of my guides. As Virtue and Van Praagh explain in the accompanying guidebook to disseminate messages, that particular card was meant to let me know that Mom would continue to help me with my life's purpose because that would be fulfilling one of her remaining life purposes.

Weeks later, on April 17, as I was once again experiencing a writing block and feeling fearful about this project - I reached out to Mom through my cards. Of course, Mom never lets me down and soon there was one card that stood out from all of the others. The card told me not to be afraid of what was to be. As I read the interpretation, heavy tears ensued. The message conveyed that all of Heaven was watching over me and Mom's influence would be more powerful than I could even imagine.

Throughout the work on this book, I have turned to my angel cards many times. I give thanks for the cards - and the messages that Virtue and Van Praagh so eloquently have written for those of us seeking to make a connection.

On May 25, 2017, I reached out to Mom again … the house was quiet and I needed to make a connection. As I sat and shuffled the cards - I talked to Mom and thanked her for the unconditional love that I now know is eternal.

It took a couple of minutes before two cards were dislodged from the pack and received my attention. The first card was short and to the point that Mom was alive in spirit, while the second card said she never misses giving me a kiss goodnight. I welled up and the tears started to flow as I read the messages behind each card. The first card explained that Mom was aware I missed her voice and presence but her soul and spirit were very much alive. The message reiterated that when I have felt her energy she was there and was also in my presence as I was working with the cards. The message behind the second card also elaborated on the happiness she received when she shared more time with me, and that the kisses were her way of offering healing energy to me.

Through my tears I looked up - knowing Mom's energy was somewhere in the room - and said thank you for those cards. For whatever reason that morning - my heart needed lifting and those two cards were the answer. How Mom knew those particular cards were what I needed to see is a mystery to me but, of course, not to her. Why? Mom knows me better than anyone.

There are so many ways to make connections with our loved ones who have passed and the Divine love that surrounds all of us - for those seeking answers it is important to try the multitude of options available and find the way that works best for you.

There is no time like the present to get in tune with your spiritual truth - and let your spiritual journey unfold. The answers will come to you when you are open and seeking to make a connection. Also, always remember to acknowledge the Divine love that created that special moment for you - and say thank you for that gift.

CHAPTER 8

Journaling

The author's journal for recording special messages.

I started journaling when I was in eighth grade - writing down stories that my mom and dad shared so I would always have those memories to reflect on.

Lori Szepelak

As a teenager - the journaling slowed to a crawl. I'm not sure why.

After mom passed and the signs started coming - I knew I wanted to write down these experiences before I forgot about dates and details. My first thought? Find a beautiful journal!

I went to Barnes & Noble and spent some time poring over a wall full of options. I wanted to find one with an angel on the cover - and didn't want to settle for anything less.

After perusing the myriad of journals nothing resonated with my eyes and heart. I walked away discouraged - and wondered where I would find an angel journal. Before I left the store I asked my angels for direction - where will I find the journal I am searching for? I was led back to the same wall of journals I had already carefully examined a few moments earlier.

Just as I was about to give up my eyes caught a glimpse of the journal pictured here and on the back of the journal it said - "Guardian Angel."

At that point I wasn't even concerned how much the journal cost - I knew it was mine.

What baffled me, however, was how did I miss it? I had spent so much time looking at all of the options - how did I miss that beautiful angel journal?

What I know for sure is that journal was waiting patiently

for me to pick it up - when my eyes were open to actually seeing it! Of course, that happened with assistance from my angels.

I always mention during lectures that signs are always around us - but we have to be open to them - and take the time to see, listen or sense their presence. While some signs like pennies from Heaven or beautiful feathers may be in our path, there are other ways that our angels and our loved ones who have passed connect with us.

Since I want to remember all of these times - I faithfully keep a journal - which you can see by the picture is a bit bulky since I keep photos, angel cards with messages, coins, and other special mementos within its pages.

Journal entries don't have to be long - just concise - so when you return to them - that memory will immediately come alive and you will embrace every detail as if it had just happened.

My angel journal is specifically for special encounters - not every day happenings.

If starting a journal isn't right for you - might you know of someone who would welcome a beautiful gift of a journal from you?

Once you - or a friend or loved one - starts capturing all of the beautiful love that presents itself - you will find it is not only comforting - but amazing to see all of the connections that are made. Just think ... if you choose not to write down all of these blessed encounters - will you remember them one day?

Our mother's Light shines - and speaks to us - every day. Never lose sight of her Light.

Are you in tune? Listening? Writing down those precious moments?

CHAPTER 9

Life Lessons from Mom

I love lists. Lists keep me organized.

When I was thinking about important life lessons that Mom taught me … I thought a list might be an easy way to keep my thoughts structured. Here … in random order … some lessons I treasure from Mom.

- Share a smile every day with everyone you meet. You never know what the other person may be going through; that one smile could lift someone's mood instantly.
- Share your bounty. Even if you have a tight budget - there is always a way to squeeze a dollar or two to buy something for someone less fortunate. Leaving jars of peanut butter or canned vegetables in the food pantry box at a church or police station are great ways to start.

- Share your love of reading. Reading is a perfect way to relax, unwind and recharge from a hectic day. Even though we always seem to have little time for ourselves - try to find a few minutes to read an inspiring message.
- Touch base with people who matter in your life. If you can't physically see them, make a quick call. With today's technology, there are also a myriad of ways to stay connected. Send a loving text to someone's phone - letting them know they are being thought of. Don't let distance be a deterrent to not staying in touch. I think we can all agree that time seems to slip through our fingers quickly as we get older and every lost moment can never be regained.
- Take a day trip with people who are important to you. A nice lunch out, or a walk, is a perfect way to reconnect with a girlfriend you haven't seen in ages. The ideas for day trips are limitless.
- Honor your spiritual nature. It may take some of us longer to grow spiritually … but the seeds can be planted early in life. Share your love of spirituality with others and then set them free to discover their own path in their own time.
- Heed your body's warning signs. On a more serious note, Mom had ignored the signs of fatigue among other symptoms and when she suffered a stroke - our family was shocked. Ever the fighter, Mom knew the road back from being paralyzed on one side wouldn't be easy … but she persevered and regained her ability to walk. In her later years, she was resigned to a wheelchair, however, she felt that the wheelchair was a better option than a cane in the event she fell. Her greatest fear was falling.

- Persevere through any challenge that comes your way. Each day is a gift we are given - make every waking (and awakening) hour count.
- Love unconditionally. There are no other words needed.

CHAPTER 10

Moms Are Amazing Women

Whether you still have precious time to spend with your mom - or only have the special memories to cherish - there is no doubt she holds a special place in your heart. You may be a mom yourself - and this message is even more fruitful for you!

Wherever your life has taken you to this point - it is no accident that this book has found its way into your hands. The message of a mother's unconditional love that flourishes here on Mother Earth and beyond may have been the answer you sought - or perhaps needed to hear for the first time.

I was blessed to have had my mom's loving embrace for many years - and then to be able to do the same for her in her last days.

When she said it was her time and she had to go - I teared up and said, "Ok" - and then she closed her eyes and the morphine drip began to slowly let her slip away without any more pain.

In those last 23 hours by her side - all I could do was keep telling her how much I loved her and that I couldn't have imagined having a more amazing mom to call my own.

If your mom is still in your life - call her, visit her, and tell her how much you love her. She will never grow tired of being in your presence - in whatever form that takes.

The bond that we share with our mothers is, of course, unique but yet there is a common thread that weaves through each of us - that we wouldn't be here if it wasn't for this amazing woman who knew in her heart you were a Divine spark that needed to shine in your own way.

If your mom has passed - whether it was recently or many years ago - the gift I give to you is that you can reach out to her anytime and she is there - in Spirit - and when you least expect it - she will come to you with an open heart and with the most loving embrace.

Once you experience that first embrace from beyond - it is a gift you will never forget and always treasure.

May the Source of All That Is - inspire you to look at a mother's unconditional love in a new way - one filled with love, light, energy and hope - each day of your life.

CHAPTER 11

Soul Contracts

Have you ever thought about our soul connection to our loved ones who have passed - or the Universe?

Over the years as my spiritual journey has blossomed - I have read several books about the soul - but never made a conscious connection until I started writing this book.

There are so many interpretations of what the soul is - deep imbedded love, Spirit yearning for more answers, Light that helps awaken us to everything we can be, a traveler seeking Ascension.

Since we are all unique spiritual beings having a human experience at this moment in time on Mother Earth, there are many ways to receive answers - including meditating and asking Spirit and one's soul to help us determine our purpose on this earth plane.

Here are some questions that Spirit suggested to me one early summer morning - as the house was quiet and I asked - what should people know about their time on Mother Earth?

Spirit's responses came quickly in this order: Why are we here at this moment in the planet's history? What contributions do we need to make before we exit to return to Spirit? What footprint did we leave for others to follow that contributed to the health of Mother Earth and all of her creatures?

Do you believe that we already possess all of the answers deep within us - in our soul - and that we only have to look inside ourselves to find the answers? I do ... now ... but it has taken me years - perhaps several lifetimes - to believe that truth.

How often have you heard of someone described as an "old soul?" Over the years I heard that phrase but it didn't resonate until now. I was even called an old soul once during a workshop on automatic writing but didn't understand and appreciate the comment. I would have asked more questions of that person - how did she sense that about me?

When we think about the soul - we can also ponder what contract might have been arranged before we arrived here - with other spirit beings from the other side. Wisdom handed down through the ages suggest that we had made a pact with our parents on the other side and agreed we would all be together at the appointed time. While that may seem hard to grasp - when we think about the infinite possibilities of the Universe - why couldn't it be true?

Lori Szepelak

These are all amazing conversations I wish I could have had with my mom - but I wasn't far enough along on my spiritual journey to think about these questions.

How often do you engage in conversation with your mom on topics like this? What if you both did a meditation together - asking the same questions - to see what responses you receive? Women's circles have emerged more prominently in recent years - allowing women who seek more spiritual guidance to gather in a safe and supportive setting. Perhaps a woman's circle gathering might make a nice gift to give yourself and your mom?

Whatever means you use to seek more soulful interpretations of your role while on Mother Earth, know that your own mom can be a magnet to help you learn and grow. Since your mom gave you life as part of her soul contract - she too wants to see you aspire to your highest self. Never miss a chance to share a special soul-to-soul experience with your mom - since you will be assisting her in her ongoing role as a nurturer.

CHAPTER 12

Saying Thank You To All Mothers

To all of the mothers on the heavenly plane - Thank You!

Your love knows no bounds - just as it was when you were giving comfort and love each day on the earthly plane.

While many of us gravitated to your open arms - there may have been some that chose another path - for another reason. Perhaps now their heart has been healed as they reflect back ... or perhaps as part of their spiritual journey ... they won't discover the true meaning of a mother's love until they return to the heavenly plane with you.

We also acknowledge that there were situations that mothers may have put their children through that were unimaginable. We don't understand why those acts have to take place ... we can only hope that all of the souls involved will be able to unite on the heavenly plane and heal from those experiences. We wish we could take the pain away for so many who have felt their lives were destroyed by their parents … we wish for them peace and love to fill their hearts.

If you are someone who felt betrayed - seek answers - especially deep within your soul. Send messages out to the Universe asking for guidance on how to address the ingrained feelings that still cling to your heart. If your parents are still with you - have a heart-to-heart conversation if you can. Know that even though the situation may never be resolved - you can then walk away knowing you wanted to make peace and then let your higher self assist you to move on.

While many may feel their angels weren't looking out for them during those trying times - please know they never left your side. As part of your "life plan" you may have determined before you arrived on the earthly plane that you wanted to learn lessons about those situations you found yourself in. Did those situations make you a stronger person today? Are you now an advocate for others who find themselves in similar situations? Were you able to grow and now can make a difference in the world for others? Only you in your own time can answer those questions.

CHAPTER 13

Mom's Greatest Gift

As months passed between writing chapters of this book and editing, I knew as I was finalizing the first draft that a message was still missing. I prayed for that message.

After months of considering several options for "what was missing" - one day it became crystal clear.

Prayer.

One of my mom's greatest gifts was a saying - *"If you are troubled or in doubt - turn your situation over to Jesus. He will always be there for you."*

When Mom passed - I lost my biggest cheerleader and go-to counselor who always had the answers. Without Mom's counsel I made a lot of mistakes which I know now were all part of my journey that would lead me to where I am today.

While I was writing this book I was diagnosed with a health

issue which totally caught me off guard. I soon found myself stressed out and probably driving everyone crazy around me.

One night - as I was closing out my day - Mom's saying came to light and I realized that I had to turn over my diagnosis to Jesus.

I said a thoughtful prayer to Jesus in the stillness of the night - explaining why I needed his help. Immediately after I prayed - the tears started flowing and my heart became light. In that moment, Jesus answered my request - I could feel it in my heart. Gone was the worry … I knew I was in the best hands.

In conversations with Mom she had said countless times she had to turn her troubles over to Jesus because her heart was too heavy. What she knew about Jesus' love for all of us she wanted to share with me so that I would realize I was never alone - even if I thought I was.

For anyone who questions whether they are alone in this world - REJOICE - you are not alone. There is so much love for each of us emanating from the Universe - know that love is limitless and we all have the ability to welcome that love into our lives.

I hope Mom's simple message of reaching out if you feel troubled - will help you one day should the need arise.

CHAPTER 14

Saying Thank You to Mother Earth too!

While we are saying thank you to mothers - let's send a shout out to Mother Earth - for everything she provides to us every day.

Living at this moment in time on the planet is a beautiful gift we have been given - and saying thank you out loud is one way to send amazing love out into the Universe. Take a few moments right now and try it - whether you are inside your home or standing outside a doorway - or perhaps reading this excerpt under a shady tree or on a beach - and see how amazing you feel.

Hear the words vibrate inside you as you find your own way of saying thank you.

My mantra is simple: "Thank You Mother Earth for all of

the blessings we receive each day because of your willingness to give us a life-sustaining planet." Will this mantra - or your own - become a daily gift to send out to Mother Earth? I hope so.

Whenever I say thank you - in whatever context it is - I am always filled with joy and gratitude.

I learned many years ago about the importance of saying thank you - from mom. Simple words of wisdom … that should be expressed with a big smile as often as we can.

How easy it is to say, "I don't have the time right now" to send out an intention, a message of gratitude, or a simple thank you. Will today be the day you decide to change that thinking and begin saying thank you as often as you can? That is my hope for you.

Saying thank you is such a simple task that can elevate us inside and uplift those around us. Perhaps too your enthusiasm for saying thank you will be contagious - and will bring more light into the lives of those individuals you touch. Whether it is a co-worker, a family member, a business associate or the clerk at your neighborhood market, just being present to them and acknowledging them will let them know you saw them in a special light.

Just as Mother Earth allows light to shine on all of us each day to sustain us we too can be a beacon of light for those around us. Start noticing the little gestures of kindness that cross your path - and acknowledge each one with a big smile and a sincere thank you. Take the time to make eye contact so that the person knows how sincere you are … and not just saying words that have no meaning. And, of course, watch how others will react to you when you return those gestures in kind. How much love and gratitude can you share each day with those who walk in the same path you do?

CHAPTER 15

A Message
From Heaven

Since I never know when spiritual connections will be made
with my Mom, during the December 2016 dream encounter
I posed one last question to her as she was slowly fading from
my outstretched arms.

I asked Mom - "Who gets into Heaven?"

She looked at me with a big smile - she looked up at the
beautiful blue sky - and said this would be the last line of
my book.

I listened intently.

"Heaven is open to anyone who asks," she said, and she
returned to Spirit.

About the Author

The author with her German Shepherd.

Lori Szepelak has been a reporter in Western Massachusetts for more than 30 years, sharing stories of others who make a difference in their communities. Little did she realize that in her fifties, she would share her own story - a spiritual journey that unfolded after her mother passed away.

She is also the author of *An Angel on My Shoulder*, published in 2010, which details how a blue aura in a photograph shaped how she sees the "other side," and *Floors of the Forest*, published in 2013, a message of how each of us - especially young people - can help preserve Mother Earth with help from the angelic realm.

Her messages and lessons learned are simple and explore what is at the heart of our existence - love.

For more information on hosting a lecture, visit her website at www.loriszepelak.com.

In keeping with her commitment to keep the love flowing in the Universe - a portion of the proceeds from the sale of each book is given to a charity - ranging from local projects to international organizations that are recognized as global leaders in helping preserve our planet.

Printed in the United States
By Bookmasters